PAMPHLETS ON AMERICAN WRITERS · NUMBER 79

John Updike

BY CHARLES THOMAS SAMUELS

UNIVERSITY OF MINNESOTA PRESS · MINNEAPOLIS

PUBLISHED IN GREAT BRITAIN, INDIA, AND PAKISTAN BY THE OXFORD
UNIVERSITY PRESS, LONDON, BOMBAY, AND KARACHI, AND IN CANADA
BY THE COPP CLARK PUBLISHING CO. LIMITED, TORONTO

FOR NADA,
WHO MAKES THINGS GROW

CHARLES THOMAS SAMUELS teaches English at Williams College. He has written on films for the *American Scholar* and *Hudson Review* and on books for the *Atlantic Monthly, Book World*, the *Kenyon Review*, the *Nation*, the *New Republic*, and many others.

⤴ *John Updike*

BLESSED with multiple talents, prolific in their expression, John Updike is doubtless a prodigy. At a stage when most young writers have scarcely identified their strengths, Updike was already a seasoned professional. Soon after graduating from Harvard, at twenty-two, he sold his first story to the *New Yorker*, joining its staff for two years and remaining a steady contributor thereafter.

In 1968, when he published *Couples*, Updike was the author of four other novels (*The Poorhouse Fair*, 1959; *Rabbit, Run*, 1960; *The Centaur*, 1963; *Of the Farm*, 1965). In addition, he had published over seventy stories, enough to fill three volumes (*The Same Door*, 1959; *Pigeon Feathers*, 1962; *The Music School*, 1966) — with another obviously forthcoming — as well as numerous reviews, essays, parodies, sketches (most of which are collected in *Assorted Prose*, 1965), and two volumes of verse (*The Carpentered Hen*, 1958; *Telephone Poles*, 1963; a third, *Midpoint and Other Poems*, was published in 1969 while this pamphlet was in press). There are, moreover, several works for children, an opera libretto, and a pageant Updike wrote for Ipswich's 1968 celebration of its seventeenth-century day. In that year, the author was thirty-six.

Prodigious as are the bare facts of his output, his proficiency is more impressive. Whatever their ultimate critical verdict, few judges deny Updike's expertise. Though occasionally drawing attention to itself, his prose is always precise and supple, equally adapted to fine emotional nuance and the painterly objectivity with which he limns the external world. In large-scale narrative,

5

Updike's craft sometimes falters, but it serves him unerringly in forms as different as the light-verse jingle and the critical essay, the dramatized meditation and that quick glimpse of character or way of life that constitutes a modern story.

Of this last form, he is a master. In one phrase, he can take us to the heart of a character, like the pathetic homosexual "At a Bar in Charlotte Amalie" (*The Music School*), whose "lips . . . were too quick, snapping in and out of a grin as if he were trying to occupy both sides of his situation, being both the shameless clown and the aloof, if amused, onlooker." Or he can make a single event telling, as in "The Rescue" (*The Music School*), where a young wife, doubtful of her husband's fidelity, is convinced of his innocence by encountering an image of loneliness, spread-eagled on a ski slope. Simply lucid, wry in its implication, such a tale is also palpable, down to the grass widow's red fingernails and the blind self-concern, emblem of her condition, with which she appropriates the heroine's last cigarette.

At his best, Updike is the detailed realist, filling his stories with facts that guarantee belief. If he must prove that some characters in "The Bulgarian Poetess" (*The Music School*) are literary experts, he inserts the right information as easily as he supplies, in *Couples*, a disquisition on photosynthesis for Ken Whitman or on architectural restoration for Piet Hanema. Ours is a period dominated by apocalyptists destroying fabricated worlds and by symbolists who take off for nowhere from nothing; but Updike offers the novel's traditional pleasures: through his insight he brings freshness to the familiar, while through his concreteness he makes familiar what was previously unknown.

In his verse, however, he frequently exploits the familiar (animals, artifacts, mundane occupations) as an occasion to display his talent for comic rhyme, or toys with the unknown by ridiculing peculiar names or by spinning fantasies based on odd news clippings. Sometimes, Updike can be witty, as in the pedagogic use to which he puts an apple:

> My child, take heart: the fruit that undid Man
> Brought out as well the best in Paul Cézanne.

Too often, he is merely cute.

Lacking sufficient gaiety or antic imagination, Updike's verse affords few smiles. When, occasionally, he attempts serious poetry (particularly in *Telephone Poles*), it is scarcely more evocative. One exception is the passionate "Seven Stanzas at Easter." Sharply phrased, this poem argues against the metaphoric conception of religious ritual and helps to explain Updike's preference for literal believers, however destructive, over men who want to make dogma comfortable.

According to the author, if even his lightest verse goes well, it gives him "a pleasure and satisfaction not lower than in any other form of literary activity." However, readers may deplore his refusal to withhold from publication work that displays little besides this delight in his technique.

Yet even in the abyss of insignificance he may lodge a nugget of perception, like this fashion note in an otherwise negligible Christmas sketch: "this year's high heels do not jounce the face but wobble the ankles, so that women walking have the tremulous radiance of burning candles as, step by step, they quiver in and out of balance." Wary of missing such pleasures, we read on; but should we forgive Updike's distributing his genius rather than distilling it for the exclusive production of major works?

In a caustic review of James Agee's letters to Father Flye, Updike hints at an answer. According to friends, Agee was destroyed by mass-media seductions that caused him to bury his talent in the anonymous sands of *Time*. But, as Updike argues, "a culture is enhanced, rather than disgraced, when men of talent and passion undertake anonymous and secondary tasks. Excellence in the great things is built upon excellence in the small; Agee's undoing was not his professionalism but his blind, despairing belief in an ideal amateurism."

Disapproving of so austere an ideal ("I would write ads for deodorants or labels for catsup bottles if I had to"), Updike can argue that his trivial or popular work has cultural value precisely because he is skilled. Moreover, despite early poverty, his youthful marriage, and a growing family, Updike did not, like many of his colleagues, seek a buffer against insecurity through teaching, editing, or other permanent full-time jobs.

Some of his "secondary tasks" are included in *Assorted Prose*: slight parodies, like one purporting to satirize a golf manual by offering minute information on how to drink from a cup, or several of those "Talk of the Town" notes from the *New Yorker* that are the literary equivalent of marzipan. But the rest of the volume is more substantial, containing brilliant memoirs, book reviews, and a masterpiece of sports writing (on Ted Williams) that shows the flexibility Updike's professionalism makes possible.

Of particular interest are the reviews. In addition to proving Updike an erudite, discerning judge of other men's work, they frequently contain valuable reflections of his own. Thus, in a piece on Denis de Rougemont, Updike formulates the relationship between two of his favorite subjects ("Our fundamental anxiety is that we do not exist — or will cease to exist. Only in being loved do we find external corroboration of the supremely high valuation each ego secretly assigns itself"), while in defending Salinger, he explains his own preoccupation with those largely spiritual anxieties that afflict the middle class: ". . . Salinger's conviction that our inner lives greatly matter peculiarly qualifies him to sing of an America where, for most of us, there seems little to do but to feel. Introversion, perhaps, has

8

been forced upon history; an age of nuance, of ambiguous gestures and psychological jockeying on a national and private scale, is upon us, and Salinger's intense attention to gesture and intonation help make him . . . a uniquely pertinent literary artist."

Besides depicting subjective experience through nuance in speech and gesture, Updike and Salinger share other characteristics. Both are obsessed with life's transiency and the power of love to act as antidote or counterforce; both are nostalgic about youth, with its honesty and illusions of permanence; and both deal with relationships that are fundamentally private.

Yet Salinger is more sentimental than Updike in presenting his subjects and themes. Though Salinger's characters may enter a never-never land, like that of the Glass family, where everyone loves everyone and not even death dissolves bonds, Updike's heroes often discover that intimacy involves disappointment, that love is itself transitory, and that the search for permanence may hinder life. In his review of *Franny and Zooey*, Updike criticizes Salinger for dividing the world into sheep (children or innocents) and goats (adults or worldlings); in Updike's fiction, contrasts are less morally stark.

Indeed, in the strict sense, Updike isn't a moralist. Though his characters may raise moral questions, Updike avoids unequivocal answers. One cannot extrapolate from his fiction a code of values, as one can, for example, derive the value of sensitivity from Salinger, sympathy from Malamud, courage from Hemingway. With the partial exception of George Caldwell in *The Centaur*, Updike's characters are likely to be true or false to themselves, more or less in touch with reality, rather than good or bad.

Nor is Updike primarily concerned to describe place or analyze culture. Much of his work is laid in a single Pennsylvania town, but Olinger could be any small community; and its mores, sparsely presented, have no crucial effect on the inhabitants. Though

9

his work expresses hostility to modern America, his charges are much less specific than those of writers like Styron or Mailer. Even in *Couples*, which treats contemporary suburbia, Updike uses place and historical moment mostly as a backdrop against which his characters interact.

But though he presents all interaction as it is perceived by the participants, Updike is also not a psychologist. Seldom does he take us into a character's mind; if he does, it is never to explore the anatomy but only to establish the perception. Often, his characters have troubled souls, and Updike himself is deeply concerned with matters of religion; but his people don't experience breakdowns or conversions, as people do in Salinger, and Updike's religious ideas can't be easily labeled, as can those of Flannery O'Connor.

As Updike says in his *Paris Review* interview: "narratives should not be *primarily* packages for psychological insights, though they can contain them, like raisins in buns. But the substance is the dough, which feeds the story-telling appetite, the appetite for motion, for suspense, for resolution. . . . Insights of all kinds are welcome; but no wisdom will substitute for an instinct for action . . ." If this term is understood to include inner and outer territory, we can say that Updike does concentrate on action, rather than on judgment or analysis. Since he is a serious writer, his action always has a point; but establishing the point is usually less important to him than creating the action. More exactly, he trusts that action, if described truthfully enough, will establish its own point, make us aware of some possibility inherent in human behavior. And since he believes that human behavior is always ambiguous, Updike wants his stories to reflect this fact.

Because he treats ordinary people doing usual things and also avoids issuing injunctions or underlining his ideas, Updike is simultaneously palpable and elusive. Therefore, critics complain that he writes beautifully but has nothing to say, neglecting to recall that, in fiction, saying can be showing. In "The Sea's Green Sameness" (*New World Writing*, 1960), Updike openly declares his confidence that reality can come to us through language: "All I expect is that once into my blindly spun web of words the thing itself will break: make an entry and an account of itself."

Because of this aesthetic program, Updike's fiction is most usefully comprehended when grouped not according to theme, setting, or character, but according to subject: the thing itself. General notions about the past, love, and faith recur in all his work, as do settings and character types; with reference to subject, his fiction may be divided into relatively discrete halves. More self-contained is the group comprising two novels, *The Centaur* and *Of the Farm*, as well as several stories that concern his own family, despite a change of names. In the second group (including his first two novels and his latest), Updike treats more varied relationships (between husbands and wives, young and old, rebels and conformists).

Within each group there are successes and failures irrespective of the author's age at composition. Sometimes Updike selects an important situation, such as the family conflict in *Of the Farm*, and treats it fully, with precision. Sometimes, as in certain short stories, he selects an episode so trivial that his technique seems merely willful. On the other hand, he occasionally inflates his subjects with gimmicks seemingly forbidden by his general aesthetic mode — *The Centaur* is a good example of this defect.

Therefore, since Updike's career does not fall into phases — does not break into stylistic halves, like Bellow's, or into ideological halves like Hemingway's — the following survey is not chronological. Rather, the autobiographical novels and stories are discussed as a group, followed by the fiction of wider range.

And since Updike's artistic development is also unsteady — unlike, say, that of Faulkner, with his "great years" and subsequent decline — the arrangement in each group is qualitative rather than temporal. Which also reminds us that Updike has only reached the midpoint of his career, a career, in competence and regularity of performance, that already promises to break the dominant pattern of American literature, whose writers peak early and then fall to feeble self-imitation. Thus, Updike's next novel will presumably be a new departure: he has announced his intention to write a full-fledged historical work on President James Buchanan.

In Updike's preface to the Vintage collection of his favorite Olinger stories, he warns his readers not to simply equate fact and fancy, but by comparing Updike's interviews with his tales, we learn that much of his fiction is thinly disguised autobiography. (In the case of "The Lucid Eye in Silver Town," a sketch first published as a story was subsequently included among the memoirs of *Assorted Prose*.) Whether we read them in *The Centaur* or in "The Dogwood Tree" (a boyhood reminiscence), whether the hero is called Allen Dow, Clyde Behn, or John Updike, the facts are always the same. The "genius" of his mother, Updike has written, "was to give people closest to her mythic immensity." Similarly, Updike uses his family to construct a myth of parents and children.

Here is the myth and its basis in fact:

John Updike was born in 1932 in a poor Pennsylvania Dutch community named Shillington, but rechristened in his fiction to mirror an attitude (O-linger). Well educated, driven by ambition, his mother apparently fails to share Updike's fondness for the town. Forced by poverty to move to the farm belonging to Updike's grandparents, Mrs. Updike seems to have welcomed the change because it kept her son from declining into Shillington mediocrity; but (in his fiction at any rate) Updike represents his father as deploring the shift. A high-school math teacher, still remembered for his unorthodox pedagogy and his devotion to students, Wesley Updike stands, in Updike's stories, for service to others as definitively as Linda Grace Hoyer (the mother's *nom de plume* for the stories she herself writes for the *New Yorker*) stands for vigorous self-expression.

Outwardly, the mother's influence seems predominant. "Consciousness of a special destiny made me both arrogant and shy," Updike's surrogate confesses at the beginning of "Flight"; and the author's early career did forecast a bright future. Elected both class president and editor of his high-school paper, Updike also distinguished himself at Harvard (which his mother recommended because of its alumni record of successful writers): he graduated *summa cum laude*, after having spent four years as the *Lampoon*'s leading wit.

For both the author and his characters, however, achievement is only part of the story. In Updike's autobiographical fiction, the gifted, sensitive young men are usually isolated from their peers and deficient in health (Updike himself failed his army induction physical because of allergies, and one friend has testified to his compulsive need for attention). Moreover, because of their mothers' fierce ambition, Updike's heroes are often made to regard love of other women as a betrayal both of filial loyalty and of their own promise.

Nevertheless, they do marry (as Updike did after his junior year), but frequently lead discontented lives. However, their author's marriage, as he indicates in the *Paris Review*, is a working partnership; and after a brief fling at art school (the Ruskin School of Drawing and Fine Art in London, which he attended on a scholarship), he began a phenomenally successful career.

Updike has said that his father's Depression-bred fear of poverty underlies his own workmanlike habits; we may conjecture that they are also supported by his mother's drive.

Of Updike's three story collections, *Pigeon Feathers* is most completely devoted to recapturing this past. But though Updike employs an epigraph from Kafka on the gradual loss of the self's sense of history, many of his autobiographical tales belie Kafka's warning that we will "scrape the very skin from" our bodies in the act of recollection. Although stories like "The Alligators" (from this volume) or "The Happiest I've Been" (from *The Same Door*) are vivid and engaging, they are too like family snapshots, of which Updike is admittedly a devoted viewer.

In his latest collection (*The Music School*), Updike includes more of these valentines, but from a piece like "In Football Season" we infer that even he suspects them of being too slight. Thus, he forces significance. "Do you remember a fragrance girls acquire in autumn?" the story begins; but this is how it ends: "Girls walk by me carrying their invisible bouquets from fields still steeped in grace, and I look up in the manner of one who follows with his eyes the passage of a hearse, and remembers what pierces him." This terminal infusion of spiritual dread (shattering a light meditation on lost pleasure) is incongruous, like a crash of cymbals at the end of a ballad.

In other pieces Updike attempts meaning through accretion. Ostensibly experiments, "The Blessed Man of Boston, My Grandmother's Thimble, and Fanning Island" and "Packed Dirt, Churchgoing, a Dying Cat, a Traded Car" (both from *Pigeon Feathers*) show instead their author's laziness. Trying to bring illumination from anecdotal snippets merely by juxtaposing them, Updike makes all too pertinent his plaintive request for divine aid ("O Lord, bless these poor paragraphs, that would do in their vile ignorance Your work of resurrection").

14

John Updike

The Centaur, Updike's third novel and his most ambitious exercise in personal nostalgia, is also an experimental work in which divinity is asked to accomplish what might better have been left to the author. Attempting to celebrate his father, Updike employs a mythological parallel to dignify the hero and unify the plot. Instead, the device proves pretentious and confusing. Though no Updike novel has received a more discordant and evasive press, *The Centaur* won the National Book Award; and although its form contradicts Updike's normal procedure, this is the author's favorite work ("the one simultaneously most adventurous and authoritative, the one that, for all its antics, cheated least, and delivered its goods most squarely"). Both facts fit an anomalous production.

On its realistic level, however, *The Centaur* is plain enough in purpose and action, though neither is sufficient for a long novel, much less one so baroque. After a brilliant quasi-literal, quasi-mythical chapter (*The Centaur's* one successful experiment), we learn that the book is Peter Caldwell's recollection of dear dead days in Olinger. As we discover from a later chapter, Caldwell is currently a "second-rate abstract expressionist living in an East Twenty-third Street loft with a Negro mistress." Hoping to make peace with a present so much less brilliant than he had anticipated, Peter tries to use sex to assuage his disappointment. But his father's memory blocks this design; as he meditates, "I miss . . . in the late afternoons, the sudden white laughter that like heat lightning bursts in an atmosphere where souls are trying to serve the impossible." The purpose of the preceding chapters is to show that "for all his mourning" this was the atmosphere in which Peter's father moved.

Ludicrous and heroic, George Caldwell is the novel's principal triumph. Science instructor at Olinger High, Caldwell thinks himself a failure, though he is such a success that, years after they have studied with him, people still recall his crucial effect on their lives. Foolishly self-deprecating, his unorthodox methods yield brilliant results. Faced with an unruly bunch of dumb pupils, he unveils creation by turning geological epochs into hours on the clock. Needing to explain the decimal system, he scoops up a pile of snow (as did Wesley Updike himself), and hurls a frigid decimal point at the blackboard. Pretending to hate his students, Caldwell in effect gives them his life — suffering ingratitude, administrative interference, and his wife's dissatisfaction with a teacher's salary — so as to minister to the mind and heart of youth. To a dumb girl tormented by parental pressure, Caldwell gives advance information on a quiz. When a diver he has coached tries but fails in competition, Caldwell alone applauds. Similarly, though he insists he is useless as a father, George both protects Peter's body and nurtures his soul.

But with youth's harsh simplicity, Peter, who is embarrassed by the man's eccentricities, frequently ignores Caldwell's marvelous selflessness. Thus, when they pick up a hitchhiker on the way to school, Peter is furious that Caldwell allows the bum to steal the new pair of gloves he had purchased for his father but Caldwell had found too good to wear. Accosted by a drunk, when their car breaks down and they are forced to seek a night's lodging, the father reacts tolerantly when the drunk tries to extort money by pretending that Caldwell is a designing pederast, but Peter finds the hilarious episode entirely sordid. In fact, the son is jealous of all who receive his father's affection at the same time that he realizes his own stature is but a reflection of their gratitude toward the older man: "being Caldwell's son lifted me from the faceless mass of younger children and made me, on my father's strength alone, exist in the eyes of these Titans."

Caldwell's complexity and Peter's ambivalence toward him provide *The Centaur* with richly lifelike material. Though it doesn't quite make a plot (moving dizzily instead through illustrative tableaux), it nevertheless achieves a sort of climax. Toward the end of the book, when they are stalled in a snowstorm and Caldwell marvels at another driver who passes without offering help, Peter pronounces a tribute to George: "'. . . there's nobody else like you, Daddy. There's nobody else like you in the world.'"

Unfortunately, this climax occurs without adequate preparation; so much of the novel deflects attention from the relationship between father and son that we don't fully comprehend or anticipate Peter's sudden inspiration. Rather too much is heard concerning Peter's feelings toward Mrs. Caldwell and of his emerging independence through a young girl's love. This too reaches a climax, but one that is embarrassingly sentimental: when Peter's sweetheart conquers his shame by accepting the sores that inspired it. Other material from Updike's Olinger stories, concerning mother and grandparents, also clutters the book, as does nostalgic recall of schooldays. Characters are introduced and dropped; relationships, like that between the Hummels, are fully established but never resolved. Characteristically well observed, these items confuse a novel already verging on obscurity.

The obscurity is caused by Updike's decision to wrap his childhood memories in the august mantle of myth. Thus Caldwell is also Chiron, noblest of the centaurs, mythological instructors of youth. Unfortunately, mythical and actual have only tenuous links. Whereas Chiron was wounded by an arrow during the centaurs' battle at a marriage feast, Caldwell is shot by a tangible form of his students' animosity. For the myth to work, Peter should be Prometheus, but he is surely no hero. Though his psoriasis is compared to birdmarks and he complains of being chained to a rock, the disease which "females transmitted . . . to

17

their children" is too plausibly understood as a psychosomatic symptom of maternal domination, and the rock is apparently the maternal power that alienates Peter from his peers.

Most serious, it is difficult to equate the end of the myth with the end of the novel. Whereas Chiron atoned for Prometheus' theft of fire by sacrificing his own life, Caldwell does not die literally. Rather, he evidently accepts the idea of death because he "discover[s] that in giving his life to others he enter[s] a total freedom." But if this is so, in what sense does the discovery save Peter? As Updike has declared, we are to understand that Caldwell will now go on enduring mortal doubt and suffering, but in that case he is merely consenting to work for his family — a laudable decision, but scarcely mythmaking.

Intended, in large part, to vouch for his father's greatness, the myth seems like special pleading. More annoyingly, it neither aids comprehension nor establishes tone. Supplying an index at his "wife's suggestion," Updike coyly confesses that "not all characters have a stable referent." Some stable referents are rather sophomoric. Thus Medusa is a study-hall proctress with pencils in her hair, and Caldwell is always making feeble jokes about the mythological parallel (for example, to a janitor: " 'Don't think I don't appreciate what a job it is to keep this stockyard clean. It's the Augean stable every day of the week' ").

Where, at last, does the mythology come from? Since we are told that the book is Peter's reminiscence, it might come from him; why then did Updike make him a painter rather than a writer? In the latter case, we could have agreed (with Updike's most generous critics) that the myth offers literary proof of Peter's final respect for his father. As things stand, Updike seems all too justified when, in the unedited copy for his *Paris Review* interview, he calls the novel a "gag."

Despite the first chapter, memorable scenes throughout, and

18

the engaging central character, *The Centaur* is not successful. Technically a sport, it must, I think, be considered Updike's most egregious example of inflation. Buried within its chinese boxes is a good short novel about the relationship between father and son and the ethics of selflessness, but that novel should not have been so difficult to find.

When Updike writes about his mother, he is more direct. In such stories, relationships are so complicated and feelings so profound that *The Centaur*'s prankishness seems to be out of the question. Coming from an obviously crucial preoccupation, these are among Updike's most subtle and powerful tales.

Like all the rest of them, "Should Wizard Hit Mommy?" (*Pigeon Feathers*) shows how little he need sacrifice actuality to explore truth. At night, by fabling their children to sleep, men confirm themselves as fathers. Protective though the gesture be, it can prove dangerous to the protector. Once in the world of make-believe, we may be attacked by buried memories from our own childhood. On this premise Updike's story is cleverly based.

"Each new story," the narrator tells us, "was a slight variation of a basic tale: a small creature, usually named Roger (Roger Fish, Roger Squirrel, Roger Chipmunk), had some problem" which he takes for solution to a wizard. One time, the narrator's daughter chooses a skunk as hero, and this initiates a revealing improvisation. The skunk's problem is his odor, which repels other small animals, so that he asks the wizard to grant him the smell of roses. But when his mother discovers the change, she returns him to the wizard and insists that he be made, once again, her son: a proper skunk. Although the other animals come to accept the skunk despite his reversion, the narrator's daughter asserts that the mother should be punished for her insistence; but the narrator, espousing filial loyalty, disagrees. Then, when he completes his paternal ritual by rejoining his wife, he shows what the tale reveals about man's fate. For as he looks at his wife's body, pregnant with their third child, he feels a surge of resentment. Unlike the little skunk, who affirmed mother without losing his friends, the adult male renounces mother only to gain a wife who cannot love him so exclusively.

Perhaps the most brilliantly written of this group (all from *Pigeon Feathers*), "Flight" is an even clearer image of the conflict in Updike's heroes between love for the mother and love for others. First-person reminiscence, it is saved from formlessness by the controlling image of flight; though it reviews *The Centaur*'s family history, it approaches universality not through technical contrivance but through the depth of its description.

"Flight" is divided into three sections. First, Allen Dow introduces himself and recalls the moment when, standing on a hill overlooking Olinger, his mother suddenly announced: " 'There we all are, and there we'll all be forever. . . . Except you, Allen. You're going to fly.' " In the next section, he gives us a highly compressed and therefore particularly effective capsule version of the Olinger legend. There follows a precise depiction of young love. After losing a school debate, the boy tastes the delight of "bury[ing] a humiliation in the body of a woman." But he also experiences the rage of a woman whose dreams are being destroyed.

Though Mrs. Dow responds furiously to her son's first love, we cannot simply deplore her anger because Updike has previously established its sympathetic basis. Moreover, her rival, Molly, is manifestly no equal. However, what really saves this story from clichés inherent in its subject is Updike's development of Allen's response. Neither cleaving to Molly as a way of freeing himself nor submitting to his mother, Allen begins to hate the girl for occasioning the woman's exposure. Thus, he starts to punish Molly with the skill of "an only child who had been surrounded all his life by adults ransacking each other for the truth." In truth, he was not yet ready to fly from Olinger, but by fighting to retain her hold on him, Mrs. Dow unwittingly forces Allen to perceive her in a new light; and this pushes him from the nest. " 'All right,' " he lets fly at her. " 'You'll win this one, Mother; but it'll be the last one you'll win.' "

Almost a sequel to "Flight," "The Persistence of Desire" presents the same young man, this time under the alias Clyde Behn, revisiting Olinger as an adult. During a trip to the oculist, where he seeks relief from a recurrent nervous tic, Clyde meets the girl, also differently named, whom he had rejected in the other story. Out of a conceited notion that he had deprived her of something special, Clyde determines, though both are married parents, to repair his past offense. What he ignores, however, is Janet's failure to participate in his self-assertive nostalgia; and Updike draws some wry humor from the distance between the male's sentimentality, so utterly self-referring, and the female's concern, so obviously sincere despite a politeness that offends Clyde.

Like "Should Wizard Hit Mommy?" this story is easy to identify with, and its meaning arises naturally from mundane details. For example, as Behn awaits the doctor, he reads, quite expectedly in this context, a medical journal that declares: ". . . the cells of the normal human body are replaced *in toto* every seven years." This is the key to his persistence in tracking Janet through the doctor's examining rooms, seeking some response to his desire. Like Jay Gatsby in F. Scott Fitzgerald's novel, Clyde covets not the girl "but some idea of himself that went into loving her." And like Fitzgerald, whose nostalgia is similar to Updike's, the author finds the right formula to express so intense and futile a need. Nick Carraway comprehends Gatsby's fervor when the distraught man casually remarks that Daisy's love for

Tom was " 'just personal.' " When Janet parries Clyde's invitation by asking him, " 'Aren't you happy?' " he responds with some of Gatsby's odd lucidity: " 'I am, I am; but . . . happiness isn't everything.' "

"The Persistence of Desire" seems the masterwork in its group because, without sacrificing verisimilitude, it offers Updike's deepest insight into the source of nostalgia. For Clyde, as for his creator, actual pleasure is less intense than remembered joy, because memory, with its power to stop time, returns to us an imperishable self. Thus, when Janet hands Clyde a note, perhaps fixing some assignation, though he cannot make out its message — because his eyes have been dilated in his examination — he can perceive the familiar shape of her handwriting. This suffices; he will not need to meet her. Placing the paper in his pocket, he feels he has donned "a shield for his heart. In this armor he stepped into the familiar street. The maples, macadam, shadows, houses, cement, were to his violated eyes as brilliant as a scene remembered; he became a child again in this town, where life was a distant adventure, a rumor, an always imminent joy."

In his fourth novel, *Of the Farm*, a tale even more limpid and natural, Updike offers a more complex consideration of nostalgia and of man's relationship to his family. Short, plotted simply enough to be classified a novella, *Of the Farm* is actually Updike's subtlest piece of autobiographical fiction. Though smaller in scope than his masterpiece, *Rabbit, Run*, it is artistically more polished, without taint of obviousness. For Updike's belief that ordinary relationships contain manifold complications, this book provides impressive evidence. In general, Updike's mimetic emphasis makes his fiction peculiarly resistant to summary; *Of the Farm* is the most irreducible of his works.

Its surface seems irreducible by being so meager. When the

book first appeared, most reviewers pronounced it uneventful, and its plot is certainly bare:

Since his mother is getting too old to care properly for her farm, Joey Robinson promises to leave Manhattan for a weekend of chores that include mowing the meadow. Returning home with his new, second wife and her adolescent son, he experiences a rivalry between Mrs. Robinson and Peggy so intense as to threaten the meetings. As the weekend wears on, quarrels break out, only to subside without warning. Melodramatically, the mother rages; suddenly "hysteria [falls] from her like a pose." The wife seems daunted, but soon she fights back. On Sunday, Joey takes the old woman to church. His mother had wanted him to retain the farm after she died; now she agrees that it be sold. Soon the city-dwellers will depart.

What does it all mean? The Sartrean epigraph offers a clue: "Consequently, when, in all honesty, I've recognized that man is a being in whom existence precedes essence, that he is a free being who, in various circumstances, can want only his freedom, I have at the same time recognized that I can want only the freedom of others." To Sartre, freedom means doing; to Updike seeing. To Sartre, we redefine our lives by changing our acts; to Updike, we change our attitudes. But for both writers, the past brings the threat of imprisonment in its potential for rigid definition.

"All misconceptions," Joey Robinson asserts, "are themselves data which have the minimal truth of existing in at least one mind. Truth, my work had taught me, is not something static, a mountain-top that statements approximate like successive assaults of frostbitten climbers. Rather, truth is constantly being formed from the solidification of illusions." The truth of his mother's life had solidified into her shared illusion of their special fate. As the novel progresses, that illusion melts; at its conclusion, Joey is able to remount the stream of life.

Like Allen Dow in "Flight," Joey had been only partly liberated from his mother's influence. " 'I've always felt young for my age,' " he tells us by way of introduction; soon we learn why. Entering his house, he habitually "resent[s] how much of myself [is] already here. . . . I [am] so abundantly memorialized it seem[s] I must be dead." Since, like all Updike's sensitive heroes, Joey longs for a kind of ongoing immortality, in which no moment is ever wholly lost, for him, maturation means decay more than growth. Looking at Richard, standing next to Peggy, the boy's mother, Joey becomes jealous, even though Peggy is his wife, for he wishes to possess in her both wife and mother, going to her in Richard's "size."

Drawn to his mother's vision of his promise, Joey has made only frail gestures of self-assertion. He married, but his first marriage failed. He denied his mother's wish that he become a poet, but he lives in the grip of poetic nostalgia. Marrying Peggy was another bid for freedom, but this too is incomplete. That his mother can so challenge his choice shows how little he has made peace with it. That he so fears Peggy's past (both in her child and the husband he suspects she may still love) shows how fervently he seeks the support of total acceptance. Therefore, desiring a perfect corroboration of his own identity, he comes home. But, as Peggy says, it is cowardly to expect either his mother or his wife to give him self-direction.

Rather Joey can only stand on his own if he frees himself from the figure he cuts in both their myths. Mrs. Robinson neglected her husband to devote herself to Joey, for Joey was, so to speak, the objectification of her own self-image. When Peggy charges her with this neglect, and Mrs. Robinson counters by calling it liberation, Joey witnesses the clash of alien perspectives. "I saw," he thinks, "that my mother's describing as a gift her failure to possess my father . . . had touched the sore point within [Peggy] around which revolved her own mythology, of women giving themselves to men, of men in return giving women a reason to live."

For a time, Joey tries to simulate freedom through the most basic fact of manhood. Conceiving Peggy as a field, he sows the seed of his possession; but in so doing, he takes his wife on his mother's terms. Making of Peggy an ersatz farm, he turns to her for sex, not love, and thus confirms his mother's denigration.

As in "Flight," Updike's hero cannot be free until he accepts the truth about both of his women; for only then will he acknowledge the change that has taken place in himself. His mother is no longer "the swift young" woman of whom he has felt himself deprived. She has "entered, unconsciously, a far territory, the arctic of the old," where her vision of his life will also die. Peggy may be inferior to Mrs. Robinson, but she is Joey's choice and now deserves his loyalty. Time has indeed passed; Joey is a man. Now he must accept a man's responsibilities.

This he does in two scenes, both of which involve the process of revision. First, Joey tells Richard a fairy tale that recalls the similar device in "Should Wizard Hit Mommy?" But in that story the teller is drawn back to his mother's self-referring vision of his character, whereas in this novel Joey uses the fairy tale to express his freedom, his ability to break out of the past. The fairy tale concerns a frog-prince with a watertight skin. One day the prince's self-delight turns to boredom until he learns of a treasure in his guts. " 'So he went down a circular staircase out of his head . . . and the lower he went, the smaller he got, until finally, just when he was sure he had reached the dungeon where the treasure was, he disappeared!' " But with the return of spring, the frog runs upstairs, throws open his lids, and looks out.

After Joey finishes, he goes downstairs expecting to perceive "some nostalgic treasure unlocked by the humidity within the stones, plaster, wood, and history of the house," but instead he smells the dampness of Peggy's hair.

This affirmation of present joy is approved by his mother after both she and Joey hear a Sunday sermon on Adam's obligation to the living Eve. " 'In reaching out to her,' " the preacher says, " 'Adam commits an act of faith.' " Woman, as Karl Barth says, is an invitation to man's kindness, and " 'kindness needs no belief.' " Joey's love for Peggy will not bring him the self-confirmation of filial love, but it is nonetheless " 'implicit in the nature of Creation, in the very curves and amplitude of God's fashioning.' "

A deeply religious woman, Mrs. Robinson apparently now sees that it would be a sin to try to maintain her hold on Joey. Therefore, she admits that Peggy suits him better than his first wife, Joan (later symbolizing the admission by asking Peggy to have a picture taken, which will probably replace Joan's). Then, after admitting Peggy's right to her son, she has a seizure, foretelling her death. But when, in her weakness, she pledges Joey to get a good price for her farm, he repays her respect for his freedom by affirming the reality of their bond: " '*Your* farm?' " he retorts." 'I've always thought of it as our farm.' "

The book's action is a record of those shifts, feints, self-dramatized assaults and stage-managed climaxes which are the universal components of family quarrels. Its power is an expression of thematic counterforce. Filled with the loveliness of primal pleasures — the farm, early mornings, one's youth — it also depicts the danger of fixation upon them. Definition requires that we keep faith with our past; freedom demands that we move beyond it. Grand though she is, Mrs. Robinson must yield to Peggy, just as Joey the boy must give way to Joey the man. But the three principal characters can only make their mutual adjustments after they have seen their situation from the individual perspectives that make it up. Subtly, naturally, *Of the Farm* performs this feat.

In Updike's less autobiographical fiction, themes from the Olinger stories recur in different form. Instead of personal nostalgia, we have nostalgia for pre-urban America. Thus the dominant characters in these stories are old men or young ones who feel at odds against the modern world. Instead of the effort to recapture one's past, we have a quest for permanence that involves religion. As in *Of the Farm*, love itself seems a religious obligation; sometimes, because Christianity has been polluted by institutionalism or diluted by a social gospel, love can seem the deepest expression of spiritual thirst. But at the same time, Updike notes the difficulty of satisfying this need. In his autobiographical stories, the hero can only recapture in fugitive moments that perfectly self-confirming love he once experienced. In these stories, the hero experiences similar difficulty through sex. Faced with woman's irrevocable otherness, he beats against the barrier between them or he pursues his ideal complement by attempting to love many women. No mortal, however, can provide the constancy and total acceptance that might hush the clock's tick. Lacking the support of faith, Updike's modern heroes can neither accept man's contingency nor find permanence through the world.

With varying success, this reality is portrayed in Updike's other novels and many of his stories. Some of the less autobiographical fiction, however, is much more casual. Most of Updike's famous marital anecdotes, for example, are usually no more complicated than his bittersweet little valentines. Trivial in situation, they are memorable only for catching a charming irony or for proving Updike's professionalism.

27

Typical of this group are stories about Richard and Joan Maple. In the first of them, "Snowing in Greenwich Village" (*The Same Door*), Updike lightly amuses. Two years after their marriage, happily installed in a Village apartment, the Maples are entertaining a female friend. Joan has a cold, but, secure in her new love, she urges Richard to walk their friend home. Though she "anticipat[es] how he would bring back with him, in the snow on his shoulders and the coldness of his face, all the sensations of the walk she was not well enough to risk," she neglects to realize that she is tempting him to be unfaithful. In "Giving Blood" (*The Music School*), one of the latest and best of the Maple stories, a rift in the marriage provides a more substantial subject. Exasperated with their mutual unhappiness, the Maples experience an unexpected rejuvenation of their love when forced to donate blood. The freshness of this experience, its external threat, brings them momentarily together; but when they deliberately attempt to prolong the novelty by lunching in town rather than at home, the old dissension revives.

Unfortunately, this story is too artful; coming to rest in a terminal pun, it reminds us obtrusively that wordplay and contrivance typify the whole. In stories whose only virtue is natural observation, Updike often spoils the effect by an ostentatious display of craft.

Far more amiable is the dramatic monologue "Wife-Wooing" (*Pigeon Feathers*). While they are both fussing with the children's dinner, the narrator woos his wife with memory; later, he tries wit. Nothing avails; she is too tired for love. The following morning, he looks gleefully at the ravages etched in her face by those duties which had made her deny him. That same night, however, although he has now forgotten his desire, she gives the cue: "the momentous moral of this story being, An expected gift is not worth giving."

Several of Updike's dramatic monologues are far more serious. Of these, the most important is "Lifeguard" *(Pigeon Feathers)*. Spoken by a divinity student who is earning tuition at the beach, this tale is a sustained conceit that comes closer than usual to an expression of Updike's fundamental beliefs.

"That there is no discrepancy between my studies," the speaker announces in his initial buoyancy, "that the texts of the flesh complement those of the mind, is the easy burden of my sermon." Then, using sunbathers as symbols, he both demonstrates and develops this thesis. Acknowledging his lust for the women he sees, the lifeguard maintains that "to desire a woman is to desire to save her," since, though sex is tragically brief, it gives man an intimation of self-transcendence. But for the swimmer unsatisfied by intimations, who is borne out to sea by time's "treacherous undercurrents," the lifeguard stands ready with two means of rescue: his swimming ability and his faith. As he sadly confesses, however, he has yet to hear a cry for help; men are all too willing now to enjoy body, sun, and sand, forgetting what Tillich calls "ultimacy." Though it is Sunday morning, neither lifeguard nor bather is in church.

This latter fact is reflected in one of Updike's best tales. Like all his successes, "The Christian Roommates" *(The Music School)*, almost documentary in detail, achieves its revelation without straining. Every year collegiate bureaucracy marries souls, in blithe disregard of their differences and vulnerability. Updike regards the effect of one such confrontation: between Orson Ziegler and Hub Palamountain.

Orson is characteristic of Updike's protagonists: bright, gangling, provincial, his inner doubts emblazoned on his face in the form of eczema. Fresh from a brilliant high-school career, he looks forward to a comfortable future when he will become the town's leading physician, like his father, and marry his childhood sweetheart. Hub is his antithesis: with his parents, who are divorced, he has little contact; arrogant and eccentric, Hub wishes to be a saint. Science he shuns because it is a modern form of *hubris*; meat he will not touch because it is produced through slaughter. Moreover, Hub has an annoying habit; at odd hours, he prays.

The freshman religious crisis is a stock situation. Equally familiar are the student types with whom Updike surrounds his principals. As usual, such material is transfigured by Updike's precise observation without losing the truthfulness that turned it into a cliché. For example, we might consider the moment when Hub disturbs Orson by describing two years of work in a plywood mill, as " 'a kind of excessive introspection — you've read *Hamlet*?' " In the time-honored manner of one dependent on knowing the answers, Orson feels threatened: " 'Just *Macbeth* and *The Merchant of Venice*,' " he admits, fully missing Hub's point.

What he cannot miss is the fervor of Hub's commitment. At first, he rather objects to the other students' smart-aleck derogation of Hub. But as soon as he begins to feel the lure of Hub's faith, he senses that he must either follow the example or make a total break. " 'I pray, too,' " he protests, " 'but I don't make a show of myself.' " Years later, when Orson becomes exactly the man he had always anticipated, he doesn't pray at all.

Among Updike's short stories, "The Bulgarian Poetess" (*The Music School*) is to the subject of love what "The Christian Roommates" is to the subject of religion. Possibly the most moving of Updike's tales, it seems to owe its power to a carefully controlled degree of personal application.

Perhaps because American life is so actual in his pages, Updike is one of our most popular authors in the Soviet Union. As a result, in 1964 he was invited to make a tour of Russia, Rumania, and Bulgaria, and from that experience he has fashioned a number of stories about Henry Bech, a once-brilliant writer whose work has steadily declined both in quality and in sales. With obvious reference to his creator, Bech feels himself in danger of "eclectic sexuality and bravura narcissism." Like Updike in *Couples,* "his search for plain truth" carries him "further and further into treacherous realms of fantasy." This decline attains some dignity only because it is pursued with much of the fervor belonging to a quest and because it has cost been his audience (here Updike differs; *Couples,* an immediate best seller, was sold to the movies for half a million dollars).

Updike's essential romanticist, Bech equates the needs of soul and heart. "He had loved, briefly or long, with or without consummation, perhaps a dozen women; yet all of them, he now saw, shared the trait of approximation, of narrowly missing an undisclosed prototype." But although he has written an essay concerning "the orgasm as perfect memory," he finds love a mystery, the mystery being "what are we remembering?"

Ironically, we are remembering what we never had. "Actuality is a running impoverishment of possibility": therefore the only truly desirable woman is the one we don't get. Meeting a gentle, intelligent poetess in Bulgaria during the final days of his tour, Bech experiences perfect love, while Updike finds the perfect words to express it. As they part, Bech places in the woman's hands a copy of his latest book with the following inscription: "It is a matter of earnest regret for me that you and I must live on opposite sides of the world." Putting this story beside "The Persistence of Desire," one has Updike's basic notion about love: either it enshrines a lost past or projects an unattainable future; in the present, it withers.

So does faith. That is the theme of Updike's first novel, his only one concerned with religion entirely outside the context of love. Though set in the future, *The Poorhouse Fair* is only an exaggerated version of the present. If modern secularism continues unchecked, Updike implies, this is what it will come to.

Weaned from the Christian vision of irrevocable human limits, modern society confesses the unsoundness of its secularism through the institutions it has produced. Designed to succor and protect, the poorhouse irritates its inmates. Since they represent disease and death, they threaten modern optimism and are therefore hidden away, depersonalized, forgotten. But what they signify should never be ignored because it can never be altered; failing to communicate with their elderly, modern men lose their unique chance to comprehend the human condition.

Death does not simplify the oldsters. Though they turn gray in its shadows, they do not lose their humanity. Though about to face last things, they are not so detached from life as to welcome prefect Conner's vision of a glorious welfare state. Will it come " 'soon enough for us?' " Mrs. Mortis asks him.

"Not you personally perhaps. But for your children, and your grandchildren."
"But for us ourselves?"
"No." . . .
"Well, then," Mrs. Mortis spryly said, "to hell with it."

Emboldened by the approach of death, such honesty makes the old enlightening. What they reveal is the avid heart of man. Because it is something they can own, they even cherish their pain. Though cowardly in other ways, Lucas refuses aid for his abscessed ear. Like Hook, clinging to his knowledge of original sin, Lucas cleaves to suffering because it confirms his existence.

This is what Conner disapproves. Seeking to eliminate man's trials on earth, the prefect wants to alter creation. Unfortunately, he is totally self-deceived. Alienated from the oldsters, he also cannot comprehend himself. When he tags their chairs, thinking to give them pride of ownership, he is surprised not only by their fury but by his own unexpected regret at losing their approval. Ironically, though devoted to amelioration, he feels himself growing old under the burden of ease: "Conner was bored. He yearned for some chance to be proven; he envied the first rationalists their martyrdoms and the first reformers their dragons of reaction and selfishness. Two years remained before automatic promotion. The chief trouble with the job was the idleness . . . He was infected with the repose that was only suitable to inmates waiting out their days."

Seeking to deprive men of suffering, secularism threatens to deprive them of all emotion. Even when Conner achieves a sort of martyrdom, he finds he lacks the belief that would lend it dignity. St. Stephen, to whom Updike compares him, was stoned for announcing the true messiah; Conner's apostleship is sterile.

Yet for all his hatred of imperfection, modern man is nostalgic about the past. This is the cause of the annual poorhouse fair, where "a keen subversive need" is demonstrated "for objects that showed the trace of a hand, whether in an irregular seam, the crescent cuts of a chisel, or the dents of a forge hammer." But while purchasing such artifacts, the younger people cheat the old artisans.

Hook, whom Updike claims to be a surrogate for his grandfather, formulates the result of modern malaise. Having lost religion, Hook asserts, the human family will ultimately decline: "As the Indian once served the elusive deer he hunted, men once served invisible goals, and grew hard in such service and pursuit, and lent their society an indispensable temper. Impotent to provide this tempering salt, men would sink lower than women, as indeed they had. Women are the heroes of dead lands."

Appropriately, Conner's mother was "excessively permissive," the non-parent of progressive education. At the end of the book, then, Hook compassionately desires to save Conner from spiritual

33

orphanhood by placing in his hands some accommodation to the limits of mortality and the agonizing fact of death. But Hook cannot think what to tell the younger man. In this novel, the wisdom of the past has become incommunicable, and the link between generations has been permanently sundered.

Like a decaying apple, *The Poorhouse Fair* exudes a tangy odor of waste. Though toughly knowing, its oldsters are both repelling and selfish, while its young people, for all their outer sufficiency and conscientiousness, are foolish and soft. In portraying this combination of crusty old age and sterile modernism, Updike creates several effective vignettes, but the book lacks a plot. As a result, the argument seems to progress above rather than within the action. And though Updike clearly sympathizes with Conner's humane intentions, the man is so self-deceived and foolish that Updike's anti-secularism is made to seem a bit pat. Individual scenes are lifelike and complex, but the book is too fragmented to be convincing.

Moreover, Updike's diagnosis of modern ills now appears imperceptive. Ten years after its publication, one can hardly believe that the welfare state threatens to eliminate all social evils; rather the reverse. Thus, *The Poorhouse Fair* helps to explain why Updike is well advised to eschew ideology; while, at the same time, it provides valuable clues to themes in his latest, less emphatic work.

Particularly those in his latest novel, *Couples*. Updike has said in a *New York Times* interview that the behavior in both novels illustrates an answer to the same question: "After Christianity, what?" Providing this link is helpful. Otherwise, as one sees in the reviews, *Couples* can be judged unredeemed pornography.

For the most part, the novel seems to disapprove of what it displays by realizing Updike's prediction in *The Poorhouse Fair* of an America in which "the population soared . . . and the economy swelled, and iron became increasingly dilute, and houses more niggardly built, and everywhere was sufferance, good sense, wealth, irreligion, and peace. The nation became one of pleasure-seekers; the people continued to live as cells of a body do in the coffin, for the conception 'America' had died in their skulls." This describes Tarbox, Massachusetts, twenty of whose inhabitants are shown as parts of one incestuous organism. Lacking real purpose, they spend themselves in copulation, ignoring morality, they also shun the outside world. Not even death has much power over their hearts. On the night of President Kennedy's assassination, they give a party.

This picture of suburban life might have been harrowing; but, as Updike confessed in his interview, he was trying for a heightened verisimilitude, approaching fantasy. In combination with his characteristic refusal to moralize, this makes the novel simultaneously implausible and equivocal. What we get then is a repetitious charade in which cardboard grotesques are unexpectedly equipped with real genitals. In one of the novel's few positive notices, Wilfrid Sheed argues that people like this *would be* shallow and absurd. Why then must the point be reiterated through 458 pages?

Though principally a portrait of doomed characters, *Couples* contains one relative exception. Bearing unmistakable signs of Updike's approval, Piet Hanema is an antique-loving craftsman, who adores the physical universe, and assuages his fear of death in the act of love. But, given his orphaned status and oral-genital fixation, he often seems an unconsciously facetious version of Updike's symbolic desire to get back to the womb. Could an enemy have more cruelly parodied Updike's obsession with mother love than the author does in the moment when Piet, without a tinge of irony, risks neck and marriage to suckle his married, pregnant mistress's breast?

Piet also fails as a hero for being too like his confreres. Updike tries to remedy this by creating two foils. Thus, Ken Whitman, whose wife Piet appropriates, is soulless, sexless, and scientific, while Freddy Thorne, who helps abort the lady's child, is atheistic, death-worshiping, and sterile. But Ken is no more complicated than Albee's Nick in *Who's Afraid of Virginia Woolf?* — which might suffice for an evening's entertainment but is too meager for a long novel — and Freddy is so often the book's *raisonneur* that it is confusing to have him also act as Piet's counter-ego.

Couples is Updike at his most wastefully evidential (one whole book, concerning the Applesmiths, is superfluous documentation). The rest is clumsily symbolic. At the finale, for example, the town church is struck by lightning, leaving intact only one emblem of God: a colonial weathercock! Though it contains a great deal of talk about God and sin, this is as close as the talk comes to providing the novel's action.

Art could have reduced the grayness, but, as Updike says, he wished to chasten his style here with circumstantiality. Circumstance we get in full measure, described in prose that vacillates between Updike's fruitiest and most flatfooted. Committing himself to banal characters, his dialogue seldom rises above their level. Occasional deviations jar like sermons in a bordello. As for the plot — when Updike gets around to it, he concocts an improbable mixture of Boccaccio and Victorian melodrama. Only verisimilitude might have supplied pertinence to this fictional Kinsey report; but in *Couples* fiction is a lot stranger than truth.

Lacking sustained insight, Updike's observation here seems voyeuristic; so much suckling so lovingly described also makes one suspect advocacy — despite all the conceptual disclaimers. Lacking order, the exemplification becomes tedious. Unfailingly vivid, filled with occasional flashes of characteristic subtlety (particularly in the last scenes of marital dissolution), *Couples* is nevertheless a travesty of Updike's most impressive book.

The hero of which, Rabbit Angstrom, also affirms life through his virility. But whereas everyone in Tarbox apes Piet, the others in *Rabbit, Run* battle Angstrom. This gives Updike's second novel a dramatic tension so grievously absent from his latest. Less trivial in what it illustrates, the novel also embodies its implications in a tighter plot. Finally, it achieves Updike's most magnanimous blend of toughness and compassion.

Slightness, mute observation, inflation of theme: these flaws in Updike can be considered personal. When he goes soft, however, he rather reflects a common contemporary problem. "After such knowledge, what forgiveness?" For the modern writer, it seems impossible to embody value. Thus, when Updike molds characters who express an affirmation, he must either elevate them with myth or unwittingly expose them, when their pretensions are refused, as mundane fornicators. Only in Rabbit Angstrom does he present someone whose value is neither exaggerated nor unconvincing.

Carelessly read, the book seems to deny this. Many of its first reviews, with titles like "Desperate Weakling" or "Down with the Poor in Spirit," judged Angstrom an example of human depravity. Ambiguous he surely is; but this is what makes him persuasive. Initially, Rabbit seems only selfish. But we soon come to admire his refusal to accept compromise or corruption. As he tells the Reverend Mr. Eccles, " 'I once played a game real well. I really did. And after you're first-rate at something, no matter what, it kind of takes the kick out of being second-rate.' " Quickened by this glory buried in his past — like Piet, the architectural restorer, or Caldwell, the teacher — Rabbit has known the pleasure of meaningful work. (Updike once said that the search for proper work drives all his characters.) Now, however, Rabbit is reduced to selling kitchen gadgets in the five and dime; yet those around him accept the MagiPeel Peeler and reject basketball as kid's stuff.

To make matters worse, Rabbit must grub for money to support a woman he no longer loves. Trapped in the small apartment his wife never cleans, he longs for the orderly home in which, like any Updike hero, he was the center of attention. "Just yesterday, it seems to him, she [his wife, Janice] stopped being pretty." Now Janice spends her time watching television, swilling bourbon, swelling with the second child she will drag up no more intelligently than the first. No wonder Rabbit dreams of his lost innocent love for his sister and rages at the girl when he later encounters Mim on a "heavy date."

Unimpressed by the obligations of work and marriage, Rabbit would like to believe that value exists beyond this world. If he cannot, he fears he will feel "hung in the middle of nowhere, and the thought hollows him, makes his heart tremble." But throughout the novel, the local church stands "gray, somber, confident," challenging him to disperse its smug darkness with an inner light. This he cannot do; he has "no taste for the dark, tangled, visceral aspect of Christianity, the *going through* quality of it, the passage *into* death and suffering that redeems and inverts these things, like an umbrella blowing inside out. He lacks the mindful will to walk the straight line of a paradox."

All he knows is self, proven on pulse and skin. Thus, like other Updike heroes, he can only seek transcendence through a woman's body. But, unlike the others, he convinces us that transcendence is what he seeks, that love infuses his sexuality. With Ruth, the prostitute he joins after abandoning his wife, "it is her heart he wants to grind into his own, to comfort her completely." When they first go to bed, Rabbit strips her makeup; as their affair progresses, he melts her protective layer of cynicism. Amidst the sordidness of Ruth's condition and Rabbit's selfishness Updike creates a real tenderness which is all the more notable for its absence in most of the author's pictures of erotic love.

This tenderness comes from Rabbit's self-assertion. Living in honest contact with his own desires, he has them to give to others. Moreover, they enable him to work his will. As he tells Ruth, " 'All I know is what's inside me. That's all I have.' " But " 'If you have the guts to be yourself . . . other people'll pay your price.' "

Ultimately Updike shows that the price is exorbitant; first he establishes the world's poverty. Throughout the book, respectable people deplore the hero, calling him a deserter and whoremaster; but what is their respectability? During his first escape, in which he drives half the night only to find he has followed a circle, Rabbit stops to get gas and is lectured on maturity by a man with whisky on his breath. Equally suspicious are the maxims of his wife's family. Though Mrs. Springer takes the tone of outraged virtue, she cares less for Janice's welfare than for the scandal. Rabbit's old coach espouses marital obligation, though he has been twisted into perversity by his own. When Rabbit repents, his father-in-law rewards him with a steady job selling used cars with set-back odometers. Every Sunday people dress for church, but their most influential preacher is the Mickey Mouse M.C. whom Janice watches religiously on television. Though society conspires to rout the Rabbit in Angstrom, it wishes merely to drive the beast underground. Instinctively clapping his hand on the soft bottom of Mrs. Eccles, Rabbit is later shocked when, at the very height of his repentance, she returns his pass. However, this hypocrisy merely explains why Rabbit cannot accept his world; it does not justify him.

A similar function is performed by the contrast between Rabbit's vital amoralism and the humanistic kindness of the Reverend Mr. Eccles. Though a churchman, Eccles is even less capable than Rabbit of accepting life or of finding comfort in orthodox Christianity. Like Conner in *The Poorhouse Fair*, he strives for amelioration, though he does so far more attractively than his prototype and his failure is therefore more pathetic.

Embodying the social gospel of modern Christianity, Eccles acts the role of frocked marriage counselor. Promulgating his congregation's values, he tries to draw Rabbit back to respectability. But because his beliefs are only a moralistic version of convention, he lacks the power to convert Rabbit's fervent soul. Instead, Eccles feels drawn to Rabbit's beliefs, which, though animal, soar higher than his own. Preaching to Rabbit — appropriately, on a golf course — Eccles is offended by the arrogance of his faith. " 'There's something that wants me to find it,' " the sinner insists. And when Eccles taunts him to produce some confirmation, Rabbit simply hits a golf ball, sending it "along a line straight as a ruler-edge," crying out "with a smile of aggrandizement . . . 'That's it.' "

Mystical in his worship of the natural universe, Rabbit's faith is still more real than that of Eccles. This the latter realizes, so when he visits the elder Angstroms he finds himself siding not with the father, who mouths society's wrath, but with the mother, for whom Rabbit can do no evil. Confounded by his own apostasy, Eccles fears for his soul. Visiting an old Lutheran minister, he is told that he is in danger of losing it. " 'If Gott wants to end misery,' " Kruppenbach thunders, " 'He'll declare the Kingdom now. . . . You say role. I say you don't know what your role is or you'd be home locked in prayer. *There* is your role: to make yourself an exemplar of faith. *There* is where comfort comes from: faith, not what little finagling a body can do here and there, stirring the bucket. In running back and forth you run from the duty given you by God, to make your faith powerful, so when the call comes you can go out and tell them, "Yes, he is dead, but you will see him again in Heaven. Yes, you suffer, but you must *love* your pain, because it is *Christ's pain.*"'" Eccles is disgusted by this rigid expression of piety, but we know how firmly Updike stands behind it not only from Hook's central utterance in *The Poorhouse Fair* (" 'There is no goodness, without belief. There is nothing but busy-ness' ") but from Eccles' final admission. "'Harry'" he confesses to the sinner he could not save, "'you know I don't think that thing exists in the way you think it does.'" To his wife, Eccles admits that he believes nothing.

By immersing himself in worldliness and seeking humane improvement, man cannot enrich his life. For that, as Kruppenbach says, he must give himself to God. But if he is incapable of such a sacrifice, he can at least take the route of substitute belief, as Rabbit does. It may also fail, and it will surely offend the Pharisees, but it can at least escape the deadness of dishonesty. By running, Rabbit comes as close as possible to the sanctity of ultimate truth.

Having considered his sanctity, we must recall his sin. More than the Springers, his parents, or Eccles, Rabbit attains sentience, but his method — total self-communion — is necessarily destructive. In nothing else does Updike so display his comprehension of life's ambiguity. Wanting us to admire Rabbit's authentic energy, Updike does not forget its terrible cost. For all Rabbit's tenderness, he is also brutal; seeking to make Ruth into a mirror of his existence he literally brings her to her knees. And by the end of the novel he has plunged her into despair, just as he has helped Janice to become a murderess.

Nevertheless, Rabbit is only speaking the truth when, at his daughter's graveside, he insists that he did not kill her. Only through a community of guilt is he implicated, but he has spent the whole book trying to escape that community; it is the others who dragged him back. Therefore, as always, he can only run away, expressing through this pathetic and desperate act, his one great insight: "Funny, how what makes you move is so simple and the field you must move in is so crowded. Goodness lies inside, there is nothing outside . . ."

Such comprehension of selfhood is not moral; but without it, morality is irrelevant. Such retreat into the smallness of one's soul is not religious; but without it, there can be nothing for God to find. Rabbit runs over others; the others beat themselves down. Despite his animality and its tragic consequences, Rabbit admits the inarguable facts of life. He is a beginning, not an end; but in a dead-end culture even so poor a beginning has its value. Therefore, his creator, scrupulously neutral till the last words, permits himself a final cry of affirmation: "Ah: runs. Runs."

Appreciating even so gross a keeper of the sacred flame, Updike expresses his compassion. Even in his meanest character, he finds something sympathetic. Therefore, the book's most powerful writing is devoted not to Rabbit but to Janice, in the scene where she drunkenly drowns her child, and thus Ruth is given the book's best passages of experimental internal monologue. Eccles is pitiable for the thwarting of his good intentions. Something may even be said for his wife, because her militant, bitchy Freudianism is a defense against the humanitarian sentiment in her husband that has no place for individual love. Updike always seeks to avoid moral melodrama; in *Rabbit, Run*, he almost totally succeeds.

Formally, the book is also a success. Its present tense and short sentences perfectly convey Rabbit's physicality. Only the plot in *Of the Farm* is more galvanic. Even the book's repetition is functional, showing Rabbit running in ever widening circles until he realizes that escape is only a straight line out. Taut and precise, Updike's prose is here firmly at the service of object, character, and event.

Only in two ways does this novel disappoint. Powerfully felt, it it is somehow less supple than *Of the Farm.* Thus we get such examples of insistence as the final appearance of Rabbit's coach, reduced to repentant mush by his high handed wife; Updike might better have omitted so blatant a validation for his hero. More serious, the book's moral poise is occasionally threatened by unneeded testimonials. So, Ruth tells Rabbit, " 'In your stupid way you're still fighting,' " though this declaration is false to their love's marvelous tact, and old Mrs. Smith, whose garden Rabbit tends, too obviously blesses him for keeping her alive.

Still, this is a first-rate novel; for without sacrificing immediacy, its image of life stimulates reflection. But, with Updike, one hesitates to conclude on such a note. Criticism normally makes fiction sound too tendentious, since criticism is the discovery of pattern whereas fiction is the re-creation of life. To repeat, it is through his power of re-creation that Updike makes his greatest appeal. Therefore, what we have barely considered — language, dramaturgy, characterization — is what most repays exploration and analysis. What I have tried to do is outline major subjects and themes as well as indicate which of Updike's works deserve further reading. Because reading Updike brings us as close as current American fiction can to "the thing itself" — which criticism can never do more than point at.

Books by John Updike

The Carpentered Hen and Other Tame Creatures. New York: Harper, 1958.
(Poems.)
The Poorhouse Fair. New York: Knopf, 1959. (Novel.)
The Same Door: Short Stories. New York: Knopf, 1959.
Rabbit, Run. New York: Knopf, 1960. (Novel.)
Pigeon Feathers and Other Stories. New York: Knopf, 1962.
The Centaur. New York: Knopf, 1963. (Novel.)
Telephone Poles and Other Poems. New York: Knopf, 1963.
Assorted Prose. New York: Knopf, 1965.
Of the Farm. New York: Knopf, 1965. (Novel.)
The Music School: Short Stories. New York: Knopf, 1966.
Couples. New York: Knopf, 1968. (Novel.)
Midpoint and Other Poems. New York: Knopf, 1969.

Current American Reprints

Assorted Prose. New York: Crest (Fawcett World). $.60.
The Centaur. New York: Crest. $.75.
Couples. New York: Crest. $1.25.
The Music School. New York: Crest. $.60.
Of the Farm. New York: Crest. $.60.
Olinger Stories. New York: Vintage (Random House). $1.65.
Pigeon Feathers and Other Stories. New York: Crest. $.60.
Poorhouse Fair. New York: Crest. $.60. With *Rabbit, Run,* New York: Modern
Library (Random House). $2.45.
Rabbit, Run. New York: Crest. $.75. New York: Vintage. $1.95.
The Same Door. New York: Crest. $.50.
Verse. New York: Premier (Fawcett World). $.75. (Collects *The Carpentered
Hen* and *Telephone Poles*.)

Bibliography

Taylor, C. Clarke. *John Updike: A Bibliography*. Kent: Kent State University
Press, 1968. (This contains errors and omissions, but, by default, it is
indispensable.)

44

Critical and Biographical Studies

Bell, Vereen. "A Study in Frustration," *Shenandoah*, 14:69–72 (Summer 1963).

Brenner, Gerry. "*Rabbit, Run*: John Updike's Criticism of the 'Return to Nature,'" *Twentieth Century Literature*, 12:3–14 (April 1966).

Burgess, Anthony. "Language, Myth and Mr. Updike," *Commonweal*, 83:557–59 (February 11, 1966).

Chester, Alfred. "Twitches and Embarrassments," *Commentary*, 34:77–80 (July 1962).

Detweiler, Robert. "John Updike and the Indictment of Culture Protestant ism," in *Four Spiritual Crises in Mid-Century American Fiction*. Gainesville: University of Florida Press, 1963. Pp. 14–24.

Doner, Dean. "Rabbit Angstrom's Unseen World," *New World Writing*, 20:58–75 (1962).

Enright, D. J. "Updike's Ups and Downs," *Holiday*, 38:162, 164–66 (November 1965).

Galloway, David D. "The Absurd Man as Saint," in *The Absurd Hero in American Fiction*. Austin: University of Texas Press, 1966. Pp. 21–50.

Gilman, Richard. "A Distinguished Image of Precarious Life," *Commonweal*, 73:128–29 (October 28, 1960).

————. "The Youth of an Author," *New Republic*, 148:25–27 (April 13, 1963).

Harper, Howard M., Jr. "John Updike — The Intrinsic Problem of Human Existence," in *Desperate Faith*. Chapel Hill: University of North Carolina Press, 1967. Pp. 162–90.

Howard, Jane. "Can a Nice Novelist Finish First?" *Life*, 61:74–82 (November 4, 1966).

Hyman, Stanley Edgar. "The Artist as a Young Man," *New Leader*, 45:22–23 (March 19, 1962).

————. "Chiron at Olinger High," *New Leader*, 46:20–21 (February 4, 1963).

Mizener, Arthur. "The American Hero as High-School Boy: Peter Caldwell," in *The Sense of Life in the Modern Novel*. Boston: Houghton Mifflin, 1964. Pp. 247–66.

Podhoretz, Norman. "A Dissent on Updike," in *Doings and Undoings*. New York: Farrar, Straus, 1964. Pp. 251–57.

Samuels, Charles Thomas. "The Art of Fiction XLII: John Updike," *Paris Review*, No. 45, pp. 84–117 (Winter 1968).

Sheed, Wilfrid. "Play in Tarbox," *New York Times Book Review*, 73:1, 30–33 (April 7, 1968).

Spectorsky, A. C. "Spirit under Surgery," *Saturday Review*, 42:15, 31 (August 22, 1959).

"View from the Catacombs," *Time*, 91:66–68, 73–75 (April 26, 1968).

Ward, J. A. "John Updike's Fiction," *Critique*, 5:27–40 (Spring–Summer 1962).

Wyatt, Bryant N. "John Updike: The Psychological Novel in Search of Structure," *Twentieth Century Literature*, 13:89–96 (July 1967).

Yates, Norris W. "The Doubt and Faith of John Updike," *College English*, 26:469–74 (March 1965).